D1414572

THE SECRET OF SIGNIFICANCE

Robert S. McGee

W PUBLISHING GROUP™

www.wpublishinggroup.com

A Division of Thomas Nelson, Inc.
www.ThomasNelson.com

THE SECRET OF SIGNIFICANCE

Published by W Publishing Group, a Division of
Thomas Nelson, Inc., P.O. Box 141000,
Nashville, Tennessee 37214.

Library of Congress Cataloging-in-Publication Data

McGee, Robert S.
The secret of significance / by Robert S. McGee.
p. cm.
ISBN 0-8499-1767-0
1. Self-esteem—Religious aspects—Christianity.
2. Christian life. I. Title.
BV4647.S43 M395 2002

Printed in the United States of America
02 03 04 05 06 PHX 5 4 3 2 1

TO MY WIFE,
Marilyn,

AND MY CHILDREN,
Faith,
Morgan,
AND
Brian

CONTENTS

INTRODUCTION

A *fter years of explaining* the principles found in this little book, I wrote what became known as "the silver bullet." The book had a silver cover and was called *His Image Bearer.* For all of its shortcomings, it was wonderfully accepted and over time became the basis of *The Search for Significance.*

Tens of thousands of people have accepted Christ and found a new lease on life as they have read *The Search for Significance.* However, there were some insights from the first little silver book that just didn't make it into *The Search for Significance.* This book brings those insights to light and also presents the other principles from a different perspective. If you have read *The Search for Significance,* you will learn much here while at the same time recognizing the basic principles. If you have not read *The Search for Significance,* I really believe God will do something in your life that is beyond what you could ever imagine as you read these pages. Those who have read both *His Image Bearer* and *The Search for Significance* tell me that as they were reading each of those books they had a similar experience: God revealed to them how much He loved them. My prayer is that you will have the same experience as you read this book.

ONE

❧ ❧

Is This Book for You?

*F*or *much of my life,* I experienced failure and rejection as if a little man who carried a hammer lived
somewhere inside me. When failure or rejection — or
usually even the prospect of either — came upon my
horizon, the little man would begin pounding away.
This soon taught me to avoid situations and people
that might create an opportunity for another hammer-
ing session.

After becoming a counselor, I concluded that God
had a solution for this reaction to failure and rejection.
I realized that almost all emotional and relational problems, as well as the identity we assign to ourselves,
have rejection and failure as major facets. If God did
not speak to these problems, which are universally
experienced by all mankind, then what else could God

1

have missed? I did not know what His answer was, but I did know that He had to have provided a key.

The question is, How do you handle failure and rejection? If any of the following seem to fit you, this book is indeed for you:

❖ Almost everyone in your world thinks you are wonderful, but that's not enough.

❖ You ruminate about the few who aren't as impressed with you as they should be.

❖ Sometimes those few are people you are closest to, or they could even be complete strangers.

❖ When you look into the eyes of others and find yourself wanting, you feel a combination of fear, anger, and a haunting sense of the lack of value in your person and maybe even in your life.

❖ You find yourself trying to gain people's approval like a beaten dog doing tricks for his master.

❖ You make decisions primarily to please others. You can't seem to say no to anyone.

❖ You may be trying to please those who have never shown a sign that they could be pleased, but you can't seem to stop trying.

❖ Some of these people you don't even like, may even hate, but you still try to gain their approval.

❖ Sometimes you call people up, knowing you are going to be put down. After the conversation you complain about them as though you weren't expecting what just happened.

❖ You may even be trying to please dead people—people who when they were alive gave you a standard that you never met, but you're still trying.

❖ You have done a great number of things well, but the failures you've had seem to dominate your thinking.

❖ Your success seems to fade with the setting sun.

❖ The more you succeed, the higher the bar is raised in order for you to continue succeeding.

❖ You find yourself limiting what you do to keep from failing.

- ❖ You go through your day checking off a mental list of do's and don'ts.
- ❖ You think some past failure has ruined your life.
- ❖ You get extremely angry with people who get in your way of achieving some goal.
- ❖ You have little tolerance for those who fail.

A young engineer came up to me after I spoke and told me that he didn't understand what I was talking about because he had never had such thoughts. He was a tall, big man and was accompanied by his small, thin wife. When these words came out of his mouth, I looked at his wife, who had an "Are you crazy?" look on her face as she watched him. In other words, if you cannot find yourself in any of the above statements, ask someone to help you.

Fears of rejection and failure are the most common fears, and they plague every person. As it is always with God, He has one solution for this problem. His solutions always work. In other words, if what you are doing is not effective, you may think you are doing something God's way, but you aren't. His ways never fail—never.

You need to realize that God knows what you are going through and even has allowed you to encounter both rejection and failure for a specific reason. This reason, which is a secret to most Christians, finds itself encompassing both eternity and time. Without understanding the larger picture, you will never understand how to be free from the emotions that can make life seem too long.

TWO

Our Destiny

It all began with God. *"In the beginning was the Word"* (John 1:1). God was sufficient unto Himself. In other words, He was complete. There was complete love, communication, and relationship between the Father, Son, and Holy Spirit. He did not have to create, but create He did.

Although we do not know everything that God created or His order of creation, we do know that He created angels. One of these angels was Lucifer. Evidently a powerful creation, Lucifer (Satan) decided that he would supplant God. One-third of the angels followed him, yet there was no prolonged struggle. God simply sent those angels that were loyal to Him to cast Satan out of heaven and down to earth (see Isa. 14:12).

Our Destiny

Adam then burst on history's scene as man was created in the image of God. How wonderful is God's destiny for man! To understand ourselves we must know why we were created:

> Then God said, "Let Us make man in Our image, according to Our likeness; and let them rule over the fish of the sea and over the birds of the sky and over the cattle and over all the earth, and over every creeping thing that creeps on the earth." And God created man in His own image, in the image of God He created him; male and female He created them.
> —GENESIS 1:26–27

Nothing else within creation has been so designed. Think about it. Consider the vastness of the universe with its countless solar systems or the fineness of the atom with its subatomic particles. None of these were meant to carry the image of God like man.

GOD'S IMAGE BEARER

But what does it mean to be God's image bearer? For years theologians have said man has intellect, emotion, and will in the same way God has these faculties. But this is such an incomplete answer, for God is so much more. Obviously, man was not created the same as God, whereby he would have all God's power and deity. But even a brief reading of Scripture will bring us to the conclusion that we are to exhibit the character of God. To be His image bearers means we are to exhibit His righteousness, holiness, patience, love, mercy, kindness, faithfulness, truthfulness, reliability, and all that is godly. What a calling! Unlike any other part of creation, we have been chosen to exhibit before all creation who He is. But it goes even deeper than this. Man was created to rule:

> For thou hast made him a little lower than the angels, and hast crowned him with glory and honour. Thou madest him to have dominion over the works of thy hands; thou hast put all

things under his feet: All sheep and oxen, yea,
and the beasts of the field; the fowl of the air,
and the fish of the sea, and whatsoever passeth
through the paths of the seas.

— PSALM 8:5–8 KJV

Consider, if man ruled the earth and Satan had
been cast down to earth, then Satan had an ever-
increasing problem, as Adam had authority over him.
In order to bring down earth's ruler, Adam, and then
supplant Adam with himself, Satan had to entice
Adam to rebel against God. Then God's image bearer,
who was supposed to reign, would fall and become
Satan's slave. Satan would then become *"the prince of
the power of the air"* (Eph. 2:2), *"the ruler of this world"*
(John 12:31), and *"the god of this world"* (2 Cor. 4:4).

This, of course, is what happened when Adam
sinned against God. Meant to exhibit the image of
God, man finds himself having fallen from such a lofty
condition. God declares that after the Fall, man's mind
became ignorant, covered by a veil, and full of vain

imaginations. Scripture teaches that we were born hostile to God, His enemy; that we were servants of sin, children of wrath, having no desire for God or the things of God.

REDEEMING OUR DESTINY

The bottom line is that natural man cannot fulfill his destiny. He is no match for Satan or even his own depraved flesh. He is so much less than he was created to be. Restoring man to be able to bear God's image and to reign is the purpose of redemption.

Of all that salvation means, you must not miss that salvation was designed to bring you back into a condition so that you can fulfill the meaning of man's original creation. Salvation was not partial. When Jesus cried, *"It is finished!"* (John 19:30), He was not mistaken. When Scripture states that we are complete in Him (see Col. 2:10), that we have been blessed with every heavenly blessing (see Eph. 1:3), and that we are now new creations (see 2 Cor. 5:17), it is not in error nor does it speak of something that is going to happen in the future.

However, the reality in the lives of most believers is that even though their redemption is complete, they are not doing well at exhibiting who God is or expressing His will. Why is this? Is it because they don't love God enough, aren't grateful enough, don't go to church often enough, or don't read the Bible enough? NO! Listen to what Scripture teaches is the reason we are not doing well as God's image bearers:

> Now for this very reason also, applying all dili-
> gence, in your faith supply moral excellence,
> and in your moral excellence, knowledge; and
> in your knowledge, self-control, and in your
> self-control, perseverance, and in your perse-
> verance, godliness; and in your godliness,
> brotherly kindness, and in your brotherly kind-
> ness, love. For if these qualities are yours and
> are increasing, they render you neither useless
> nor unfruitful in the true knowledge of our

Lord Jesus Christ. For he who lacks these qualities *is blind or short-sighted, having forgotten his purification from his former sins.*

—2 PETER 1:5–9, *emphasis added*

What are these qualities of moral excellence, knowledge, self-control, perseverance, godliness, brotherly kindness, and love? Are these not part of the image of God? Notice the reason given if these qualities are not in your life, if you are not bearing God's image. It is because you have forgotten something: *the purification from your sins.* When were you purified from your sins? It was at your new birth, right? It was when you were redeemed, when you were born again a new creation. Therefore, you have forgotten something or have not seen something clearly about your new birth:

For if anyone is a hearer of the word and not a doer, he is like a man who looks at his natural face in a mirror; for once he has looked at himself and gone away, he has immediately forgotten what kind of person he was.

—JAMES 1:23–24

What is it that the hearer "but not the doer" sees? It was his natural face. But what did the face look like?

But we all, with unveiled face beholding as in a mirror the glory of the Lord, are being transformed into the same image from glory to glory, just as from the Lord, the Spirit.

—2 CORINTHIANS 3:18

James is simply saying that if we find ourselves hearers of the word and not doers, we have forgotten who we are now because of our redemption. Proverbs 23:7 states, *"As [a man] thinks in his heart, so is he"* (NKJV). You will act consistently with who you think yourself to be. Is experiencing myself as a new creation simply accepting who I am now because of redemption? No. Simply accepting the truth of who you are will not change you. Truth that is not used to confront specific individual deception creates only the illusion of change.

The truth lies on top of the deception until the pressures of life demonstrate that deception has not been laid aside. You will fall back into your old ways of thinking. You may even begin to question the validity of the truth you had previously accepted. Romans 12:2 states, *"And do not be conformed to this world, but be transformed by the renewing of your mind."* Furthermore, we are told in Ephesians:

> In reference to your former manner of life, you lay aside the old self, which is being corrupted in accordance with the lusts of deceit, and that you be renewed in the spirit of your mind, and put on the new self, which in the likeness of God has been created in righteousness and holiness of the truth.
>
> — EPHESIANS 4:22–24

In order to know how to lay off the old man, not to be conformed to this world, but then to be renewed and put on the new self, we must know how we were deceived. Again consider, Satan targeted Adam in order to overthrow Adam's rule over creation, including Satan himself. Yet, hasn't God given believers specific marching orders regarding such authority and rule?

> Behold, I have given you authority to tread upon
> serpents and scorpions, and over all the power of
> the enemy, and nothing shall injure you.
>
> —LUKE 10:19

Do you see it? We are back to our original purpose. We are to enforce God's rule on this earth through prayer, spiritual declaration (confronting Satan by the authority of the Lord Jesus Christ), and Spirit-led action. One of Satan's greatest concerns is that you might find out who you are. The believer, because of his union with Christ, is the most powerful created creature. He has the power of God for the purpose of bearing God's image and enforcing God's rule.

THE SECRET OF SIGNIFICANCE

SATAN'S DECEPTION

If believers really knew who they were, Satan would have considerably more trouble than he does. Satan does not know who is going to accept Jesus and who isn't; therefore, Satan simply deceives the entire human race. Remember, Satan's goal is to deceive you so that even if you accept Jesus, you will not accept, and therefore experience, the new creation you have become. This keeps you from interfering with his activities.

Satan accomplishes his goals by teaching us a method for determining who we are. That method is to believe that our performance is simply a reflection of who we are or that we are what others say we are. By this method, if I fail, that means I must be a failure. If I act like a jerk, it means I must be a jerk. By this method, if certain important others think I'm a jerk, it means I must be one. The motto is, "I am what I do and what others think of me—no more, no less." In other words, Satan's lie to us is this:

Our Identity = Performance + Others' Opinions

This is the very reason that a sinner can accept Jesus, become a saint, and fall back into acting like a sinner. Few Christians have changed their way of determining who they are even after their new birth. How about you? Consider this exercise: Think of three good things about yourself. Now think of three bad things about yourself. The answers I get to the positive exercise are, "Well, I am honest, trustworthy, a good mother," and so on. The negative exercise is answered, "Well, I am a little lazy, not a good witness, not very obedient to God." Notice these are all performances, even though I asked about who you were (as a person), not what you do (your performance). It is even difficult to refer to yourself without referring to some performance because you have been so conformed to Satan's world.

GOD'S SOLUTION

Would it not be reasonable that our loving heavenly Father would make us so that we could not rest easy in

Satan's trap? Would it not be reasonable that He would make us so that we would experience enough discomfort that we would decide to forsake Satan's system and accept God's plan? That is exactly what happened.

Man is made with a reflex to evaluate himself. If his evaluation of himself is positive, then he feels good; but if his evaluation turns negative, then harsh emotional pain follows. Satan's system of self-evaluation produces destructive emotional pain in our lives. Almost all the emotional pain you experience can be traced to this problem.

The two great emotional pains in our lives are the sense of failure and the sense of rejection. Mental difficulties ranging from depression to schizophrenia to neurosis to nervous breakdowns can all be traced to evaluating ourselves on the basis of what we do and what others say about us.

We are conformed to this world and are experiencing the unavoidable emotional pain that follows. The solution is for us to accept who we are now because of our redemption through Christ and then apply that truth to the specific, individually experienced deception in our lives. Not only does this release us from the misery of the sense of failure and rejection, but we will then be able to take our place as enforcers of God's will in the world. This takes both diligence and honesty with God.

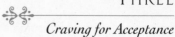

THREE
Craving for Acceptance

We *would expect* a loving God to create a situation so desperate that if we used Adam's plan instead of His plan we would find ourselves in misery. If He had not made the results of Adam's alternative so distasteful, people would never turn to God. A longer look at the results of Satan's lie that *Our Identity = Performance + Others' Opinions* will demonstrate how devastating the results are.

Fear and shame are products of the losing formula. Fear of rejection immobilizes millions. Having valued yourself poorly due to others' having rejected you, you soon become wary of certain relationships. You may find yourself defenseless against rejection, as it comes with such variance of intensity and presentation. It may be a disgusted look, the ignoring of your presence, or a cold tone of voice. It may be someone's refusal to accept anything you do as adequate or a constant comparison of your inadequacies with someone else's adequacies. It may be open hostility or the unfaithfulness of a spouse. Rejection surrounds us. A day without encountering some form of rejection is indeed rare.

THE ROOTS OF REJECTION

Rejection is the negative reflection of another's opinion of you. It communicates primarily a depreciation of you. Rejection or criticism of your person is designed for two purposes. First, this negative opinion of you is used for "motivation." Knowing that others generally have no defense against personal criticism, people can inflict pain without laying a hand on the targeted person. The idea is that in order to avoid this pain in the future the victim will cease to do or begin doing certain activities. This method works to the degree that future contact with the victim is assured. If the victim can be kept near, it works fairly well.

Sue cried uncontrollably. Bill had left her and showed no signs of ever coming back. She felt remorse over her past incessant criticism of him. Sue's system of beating him down until Bill did what she wanted him to do had worked for fifteen years. Now that Bill had left, his exhilaration, due to freedom from Sue's nagging, made it extremely unlikely he would ever return.

Many misguided preachers use personal criticism (guilt) as a primary means of motivation. For their churches to remain at the same level of attendance, they must continually get new members. There is a percentage of people who leave the church, never to return. They feel worse when they leave than they felt when they entered. The preachers perceive the people who leave as just sinners who could not stand the heat. These preachers fail to note that those who were attracted to Jesus in the first place were people who were laden with sin. God never uses guilt (condemnation of the person) for correction of behavior.

Rejection is also used to keep others away. When Harry was six, he lived with his father after his parents divorced. It wasn't so much that his father wanted him as it was that his mother didn't have time for him. His mother saw Harry about once a year. Soon after the divorce, Harry's father married a woman who already had three children. His stepmother resented having to put up with Harry. She always favored her children over him. Harry's father was a weak man who out of fear of losing this wife allowed her to do as she pleased.

Harry married Barbara when he was twenty. Their courtship was wonderful. It seemed that he had finally found someone who loved him. Thinking they could determine how married life would be for them, they lived together for six months prior to marriage. But soon after the marriage, something strange began to happen in Harry. Living together had created the illusion that they had sampled married life. They were not aware that major emotional components within marriage don't begin until the commitment of marriage has been made. In other words, there is a barrier as to the closeness people can achieve prior to marriage.

Few realize such a barrier exists, but without commitment to the finality of marriage, intimacy is just an illusion. Now that Harry was married to Barbara, the barrier to true personal intimacy was removed. He began to feel anxious. Something told him that he needed more space. Barbara worshiped the ground he walked on. She wanted to make up for all the misery he had experienced. But when he pulled back from her love, she was crushed. Harry had experienced the pain of rejection all his life; now he was inflicting it on the one he loved.

Many times the angry, critical person is just trying to push those who could hurt them away. For whatever reason and to whatever degree we have experienced rejection, a fear of experiencing that pain again can have profound effects on us. Emotional pain can be more profound than other types of pain. Early in life we learn how to deal with injury and illness, but because emotional pain is perceived as a sign of weakness, very little is said about dealing with it.

OUR FEAR OF REJECTION

Our fear of rejection exists only because we evaluate ourselves by others' opinions. You evaluate yourself because God has placed an absolute need in your life to look within and find worth in the person you are. His solution to this need will bring you into "bearing His image" and exhibiting His glory to this poor and dying world. Adam's solution of "I am what others think of me" brings not life, but death. It does not bring freedom to serve the Lord, but bondage and servitude to man. As Proverbs 29:25 says, *"Fear of man brings a snare."*

You may have always judged your person by what you and others have thought of your performance. Anytime your performance was unacceptable, you felt you were unacceptable. You may have said something like this: "I must be accepted by and pleasing to certain others in order to feel good about myself, and if others don't approve of me I can't approve of myself."

Another way of saying this is, "When certain others judge me they must find me acceptable in order for me to feel good about myself." Some related statements are: "I just can't stand it when you're mad at me." "You've got to love me." "I'd just die if he ever left me." "It killed me when he married her so soon after our divorce." "I can't stand that disgusted look on his face." "I'll never be able to face him again."

If you did something you consider really terrible, how would those you know feel about you? Most likely they would feel the same way you would feel about yourself. Whether you're talking about not quite meeting some performance standards or failing miserably, the basis for your judging your self-worth is probably the same: man's opinion. A major problem arising from having to be adequate in order to believe you have worth is a rules-dominated life.

You may know someone who has a set of rules for everything.

These individuals always focus their attention on their performance. Mel was an extreme case. He divided his day into fifteen-minute time frames. He literally knew what he would be eating each Tuesday at noon three weeks in advance. Instead of his "disciplined" lifestyle bringing him contentment, Mel was miserable. He longed to turn off his mind, which, like an army sergeant, commanded him through his day. Mel literally regulated himself almost to death.

THE IMPORTANCE OF RELATIONSHIPS

The focus of the gospel is on relationship, not regulations. Jesus' exercise of His Lordship is dependent on our attending to His moment-by-moment instruction. Focusing on rules to relegate your life sends you to the prison of self-introspection. If you have to be adequate (meet certain standards) in order to feel good about yourself and want to condemn yourself when you fail badly, then your cell awaits you.

How many hundreds of times have you faced

failure? Therefore, to some extent, you will have internalized the following sentence into your belief system, and you will hold to it with amazing tenacity: "I must have acceptance, respect, and approval in order to have self-worth (if not by almost everyone, at least by significant others)."

Many of us have been controlled by our parents for so long that all it takes is a pair of pursed lips or one raised eyebrow to make us feel unacceptable. "You're not going to wear that, are you?" "Never mind, I'll do it myself!" "You were always so impetuous." "John, all your brothers and sisters will be here, so try to be on time for once in your life!" Even gentle reminders can give us an out-of-step-with-the-family feeling. And who can resist such a sure-fire rejection "arouser" as a mother saying, "Unlike with your children, when Nancy's kids come to visit, I can just sit back and relax."

Sometimes a child reaches adolescence with a keen lack of acceptance. This can produce an insatiable craving for the acceptance and approval of others. Furthermore, a craving for acceptance is often compounded by an inability to relate with others in a relationship of depth. You can be assured that your lack of ability to give and receive love is in direct proportion to the amount of rejection you experienced as a child. You will not express love because you feel self-conscious and inept, and you will not accept love from others because you fear that it will be withdrawn. Actually, you may not know how to do either. You can't give what you have never received. If you can't adequately give and receive love, you will find it equally difficult to trust. Lacking the ability to give love, to receive love, and to trust, you will tend to reject others or to keep them at a distance.

You may find it difficult to reveal and give yourself to close personal relationships. Rejection incapacitates us for deep relationships. At the same time it produces in us an insatiable craving for acceptance. Impaled on the horns of this dilemma, we feel alone and unacceptable. A renowned psychiatrist, Erich Fromm, said, "The deepest need of man is the need to overcome separateness, to leave the prison of his aloneness."

Billy could not escape the sense of rejection he felt

when he was sober. An orphan, his adopted parents placed ridiculous demands on him. Too young to understand his "father's" questions, he would be beaten until bloody. His "mother" would laugh at him and tell him they were going to take him back to the orphanage unless he "smartened up." Billy could escape the enveloping pain of their rejection only inside a bottle of booze. Billy's only chance was to give up trying to please his parents and deal with the offenses and rejection from the past. Scripture enjoins him to do so:

> For am I now seeking the favor of men, or of God? Or am I striving to please men? If I were still trying to please men, I would not be a bond-servant of Christ.
>
> —GALATIANS 1:10

Here we see the apostle Paul drawing the line. You can either seek the favor of men or be a bond-servant of Christ. You are going to be someone's slave. Who will your master be—man or Jesus?

FOUR

The Salvation Solution

The *satanic/adamic formula* of **Our Identity = Performance + Others' Opinions** results in four false beliefs:

The Performance Trap

❖ *I must meet certain standards to feel good about myself.*

The Approval Addict

❖ *I must be approved by certain others to feel good about myself.*

The Blame Game

❖ *Those who fail (including myself) are unworthy of love and deserve to be punished.*

Shame

❖ *I am what I am; I cannot change; I am hopeless.*

Absolutely no one has ever escaped the destructive impact of this formula and these false beliefs. God made sure no one could. Recall, He placed a monitoring reflex within us that always is aware of our identity and corresponding worth.

God intends that there is but one way to escape this problem—to accept Christ and to live in the new identity that He gives you. This circumstance is a gift from God. For what good would it be for a person to live a life comfortably without understanding his need for salvation? And how much of a waste would it be for a person to accept Christ but never experience her new identity this side of heaven?

God's plan is centered in the Cross. To understand this plan you must understand the meaning of four major doctrines of Scripture.

PROPITIATION

Scripture teaches that Jesus is the propitiation for our sins:

> By this the love of God was manifested in us,
> that God has sent His only begotten Son into
> the world so that we might live through Him. In
> this is love, not that we loved God, but that He
> loved us and sent His Son to be the propitiation
> for our sins.
>
> —1 JOHN 4:9–10

To "propitiate" means to satisfy the anger and wrath of someone you have wronged. To appreciate propitiation, you must realize three factors.

First, your performance over the course of a lifetime is extremely sinful. That which is not of faith is sin (see Rom. 14:23). Prior to Jesus, everything you did was sinful for it could not have been of faith. Even our good deeds were as filthy rags to Him (see Isa. 64:6). Being realistic about your performance, you must admit you have sinned thousands of times even after you accepted Jesus. Therefore, in your lifetime you will have wronged God millions of times, counting all your sins before and after accepting Jesus.

Second, the problem with our being so sinful is that God is absolutely holy. It took only one sin to separate Adam from Jehovah. God is holy in that He is absolute purity and perfection. There is absolutely nothing unholy in Him. *"God is light, and in Him there is no darkness at all"* (1 John 1:5). Therefore, since God is holy, He cannot overlook or compromise sin.

For God to condone one sin would defile His holiness instantaneously, like smearing a white satin wedding gown with black tar. He reacts in anger and wrath to make known His aversion to sin, and He vindicates His holiness by punishing. God declares, *"The wages of sin is death"* (Rom. 6:23).

Third, God is not only holy; He is also a God of love. In His holiness God condemned sin. But in the most awesome display of love the world has ever seen, God sent His only Son to die for our sin. God propitiated His own holy nature. Thus, He can accept us without doing any injustice to His holiness.

In the case of all other gods throughout history, man has had to appease and propitiate his gods by sacrificial deeds. But our God sacrificed His Son for the propitiation of His own holy nature. What awesome love!

Look again at the verse we are discussing:

> In this is love, not that we loved God, but that He loved us and sent His Son to be the propitiation for our sins.
>
> —1 JOHN 4:10

Who can measure the fathomless depth of the love that sent Jesus to His cross?

With our performance being so sinful and God being so holy, the fact that our person becomes satisfactory to God makes propitiation awesome. Jesus' propitiation was for our sins—your sins—past, present, and future. The death of Jesus keeps us satisfactory to a God who couldn't stand us if we had even one solitary sin on our record, no matter how small that sin might be.

The emphasis of 1 John 4:10 is not only on propitiation, but also on the reason for His sending His only begotten Son. To simply say that it was out of love does not seem to do justice to what the Father did.

Experiences with my own children have brought me to a partial appreciation concerning the love it took for the Father to send the Son He had loved and communed with throughout eternity. The Father could not escape witnessing His Son's mistreatment, the scourging and the beating prior to the Cross. He could have spoken and ended the whole ordeal; yet He kept silent as He looked down through time and saw you individually. Confronted with the suffering of His Son, He chose to let it continue so you could be saved. What an expression of love with unsearchable depth!

However, the pain of the Cross to both Jesus and the Father was small compared to that strategic moment in time when the Father collected the entire wrath you deserve and placed it on Jesus. He knew the hurt and pain His dearly Beloved would have to bear; yet He completed the act, just because He loves you. Now, nothing stands in the way of that love.

Recall your experience of being loved. Your lover

adored you, wanted to be with you. You didn't have to perform; just being you was enough. The thought of that one selecting you to love was intoxicating. All other facets of life seemed to diminish. The person loved you. That person's love soothed your soul and satisfied your inner longings.

If a human lover can make you feel this way, consider how much greater joy the heavenly Father's love can bring. You have never truly experienced the love of the Father unless you realize it supersedes any experience of being loved by another man or woman.

Your Father adores you. He longs for time with you. He loves being loved by you, but He knows you can love Him only if you are experiencing His love for you.

Propitiation means you are satisfactory and you are completely loved!

Many Christians view their heavenly Father as if He were like a man I know of named Mike. Now Mike adored and proudly spoke about his fine son as long as the boy performed with his abilities and honored his father's name. But when the son went astray and was maimed and wasted, Mike no longer wanted to have anything to do with him. He was willing to provide for his physical needs, but from fear of what others would say about him, he had the son's name changed so that his own wouldn't be disgraced.

Too many think that God is thrilled when you accept Jesus and are born into His family and that He is proud of you as long as you perform. Actually, many think that the more they perform, the happier God is with them. To them, He's sort of like management at the factory. If you produce, they love you; if you don't produce, they fire you. And of course if you really foul up, God is going to put you on the shelf somewhere and take care of your needs only because He has obligated Himself to do that. Only the beautiful, producing Christians are sitting around His table, eating His food. What an ugly, distorted view of our heavenly Father Christians hold.

In reality, He loves you, and not a moment goes by that He isn't thinking loving thoughts about you. You are His child. As one of His children, you are individually special to Him, just because you are His.

Propitiation, then, means Jesus has satisfied the Father with His death. And the only explanation we have in Scripture for His going through it all is just because He loves you. The truth of propitiation is the first major aspect of your identity. Confess it as you read:

❖ *"Because of propitiation, I am deeply loved of God."*

JUSTIFICATION

Now we will examine the second great doctrine that declares our worth: justification. As Romans 5:1 tells us, *"Therefore having been justified by faith, we have peace with God through our Lord Jesus Christ."*

Justification is the judicial act of God by which He declares you free from the guilt of sin. All the sin you can ever commit has already been forgiven.

I once heard a radio preacher warn, "Someday you are going to die, then God is going to flash all your sins upon a giant screen in heaven for all to see." He went on to describe how we will recoil in shame as all the secret sins of our lives are projected on that screen. Is that the bright prospect of heaven? No, to forgive is to forget. Our justification means our sins are forever forgotten: *"And their sins and their lawless deeds I will remember no more"* (Heb. 10:17).

However, justification means more than being forgiven, as marvelous as that is. God forgives your sinfulness and provides your righteousness. Righteousness is the worthiness to stand in the presence of God without any fear of personal condemnation. God imputes to you the righteousness of Christ.

Therefore also it was reckoned to him as righteousness.

Now not for his sake only was it written, that it was reckoned to him, but for our sake also, to whom it will be reckoned, as those who believe in Him who raised Jesus our Lord from the dead, He who was delivered up because of

our transgressions, and was raised because of
our justification.

—ROMANS 4:22–25

To "reckon" as righteousness means that God attributes or applies the righteousness of Christ to your person. As an example, some have said: "It is as if God opens the heavenly ledger and credits the righteousness of Christ to your account." But this example falls short, for it seems to imply that God treats you as if you are righteous even though you are not—because some heavenly ledger is balanced somewhere.

No, you *are* righteous. God has actually attributed the righteousness of Christ in direct application to your person. It does not do God's work justice to say that God merely sees you through Jesus, as if Christ is a divine filter, so that God sees you as righteous because He sees you through Christ. No, God made an application the first instant you received Christ, and not for one moment do you cease to be anything less than as righteous as Jesus Christ.

God works by "fiat," meaning that He can create something out of nothing simply by declaring it into existence. God spoke and the world was formed. He said, "Let there be light," and light appeared. In the same sense, and with the same result, God declared you justified: forgiven and righteous. To say otherwise is to look at a cloud God changes into a rock and call it a cloud-rock. No, if God changes a cloud into a rock, it will be a rock even though it used to be a cloud. I used to be a sinner; now I am righteous. Romans 5:1 describes believers as *"having been justified,"* a statement in the past perfect tense.

In the work of justification, then, you receive the righteousness of Christ, the One of whom God said, *"This is My beloved Son, in whom I am well-pleased"* (Matt. 3:17). You have this same righteousness, which is well pleasing to God. This tells you something, which you can confess, about yourself as a Christian person: "I am fully pleasing to God." Your person is fully pleasing to God because He cannot be displeased with the righteousness of Christ, which you have received. Add this to your previous confession and verbalize it even as you read:

- ❖ *"Because of propitiation, I am deeply loved of God."*
- ❖ *"Because of justification, I am fully pleasing to God."*

When God chose to redeem you so that you could relate to Him and rule for Him, He did not go partway. He did not make you partially righteous or with righteousness that could be affected by your performance. The Cross is so significant and efficient that it keeps a child of God holy and righteous even in the midst of sin. This is not to depreciate the inherent destructiveness of sin, but to glorify the indescribable sacrifice of Jesus.

RECONCILIATION

I do not know of any biblical tenet more neglected in its practical application than the third doctrine we will consider: reconciliation. The Colossians reference to this doctrine reveals its application to you as a person:

> And although you were formerly alienated and
> hostile in mind, engaged in evil deeds, yet He
> has now reconciled you in His fleshly body
> through death, in order to present you before
> Him holy and blameless and beyond reproach.
>   —COLOSSIANS 1:21–22

Relish those last words: *"holy and blameless and beyond reproach."* God sees you like this now. This is not merely a reference to your future standing; it describes your present state.

As the verses show, you once were alienated, but now you have been reconciled and are accepted as holy, blameless, and beyond reproach. This tells me something else about you as a person: You are totally accepted by God!

Joan had a great deal of trouble thinking of herself as acceptable. Three years into her marriage she committed adultery. There was a lot of hurt involved, but God forgave her and her husband forgave her. Yet, she could not forgive herself. After four years she still could not forget what she had done. Her mind was infested with guilt. Finally, I became a little frustrated with her and said, "Well, to hear you talk, one would think that you think God will never see you the same as a person because of what you have done." "That is right," Joan replied. "I don't think He ever will."

So I asked Joan this probing question: "Is there any sin so filthy that it can make a Christian less acceptable to God as a person?" To say that this is true is to say the Cross is insufficient. If so, God blundered at Calvary, and the Bible is in error when it says:

> For he forgave all your sins . . . the list of his commandments which you had not obeyed. He took this list of sins and destroyed it by nailing it to Christ's cross. In this way God took away Satan's power to accuse you of sin.
> —COLOSSIANS 2:13–15 TLB

THE SECRET OF SIGNIFICANCE

This line of reasoning from the Scripture might appear new. However, I don't believe the question would seem like a new teaching if I had worded the question like this: "Is there any sin so filthy that it can prevent a Christian from getting to heaven?" I believe most Christians would answer a resounding "no" to this. A believer is eternally secure. Once saved, he is always saved, for heaven is a certainty (see 1 Pet. 1:3–5). However, if there is no sin that can prevent a Christian from getting to heaven, then no sin can hinder your personal relationship with God either.

Salvation is not a ticket to heaven when you die. Salvation, in its very essence, is a relationship, a person-to-person relationship. God received you into a personal relationship the moment you placed your faith in Christ. God and you are united in an eternal and inseparable bond (see Rom. 8:38–39).

You are born of God in the most indissoluble union, as joint heir with Christ. So ask yourself, "Is there any sin so filthy that it can make a Christian unacceptable as a person to God?" To say "no" is not presumptuous, but evidence of God-honoring faith in a blood-sealed warrant, with the Holy Spirit as your earnest (see Eph. 1:13–14).

On the other hand, is there anything a Christian can do to make himself more acceptable to God as a person? No! If there is, then the Cross is insufficient. If you can do anything to make yourself more acceptable to God, then Christ either lied or was mistaken when He cried out on the cross, *"It is finished!"* (John 19:30). In that case, what He should have said was, "It is almost finished, and if you live a perfect life, you and I together might get you saved."

Since you have a finished redemption, it is the height of pride to think your own good works can make you acceptable to God. The Bible speaks to the contrary: *"Not by works of righteousness which we have done, but according to His mercy He saved us"* (Titus 3:5 NKJV).

Reconciliation means you are totally acceptable to God—just as you are right now. Nothing needs to be changed, because you're not accepted for what you're going to be, but for who you are because of Jesus. Ten thousand years of heaven will not make you even slightly more acceptable to God. Jesus' death makes you acceptable to Him.

Add the truth of reconciliation as the third major aspect of your identity. Confess it as you read:

- ❖ *"Because of propitiation, I am deeply loved of God."*
- ❖ *"Because of justification, I am fully pleasing to God."*
- ❖ *"Because of reconciliation, I am totally accepted by God."*

God is not in the people-patching business. He doesn't just patch you up. He makes you better than new. Imperfection could not relate intimately with perfection. Only perfection could carry out God's rule over Satan.

Something about you was made perfect because of the Cross. *"For by one offering He has perfected for all time those who are sanctified"* (Heb. 10:14). According to this verse, you have been perfected forever.

What is it about you that has been made perfect? It is certainly not your performance. Indeed, unless you learn to differentiate between your person and your performance, the Bible will seem to contradict itself.

For example, the same book often seems to teach apparent contradictions. One passage says you are already perfect: *"He has perfected for all time those . . ."* (Heb. 10:14). Another passage says you are still being perfected: *"Let us press on to maturity [perfection]"* (Heb. 6:1). Another passage says you are already completed: *"In Him you have been made complete"* (Col. 2:10). Still another passage says you are yet to be completed: *"that we may present every man complete in Christ"* (Col. 1:28). But these are not contradictory passages. In each case, the context indicates that the first verse has to do with your person and the second with your per-formance.

REGENERATION

God's perfection of your person has to do with the doctrine of regeneration: *"He saved us . . . according to His* mercy, *by the washing of regeneration and renewing by the Holy Spirit*" (Titus 3:5).

Regeneration, our fourth doctrine, is the renewing work of the Holy Spirit by which a Christian literally becomes a new person. Your regeneration took place the instant of your conversion to Christ. The Holy Spirit effected a spiritual birth within you. God regenerated you. You experienced more than a revolution or change of direction. You experienced involution, the communication of new life.

The part of you that the Holy Spirit regenerated is your human spirit. The Holy Spirit has energized your inner spirit with new life. Jesus called it a "new birth" in John 3:3–5, saying that it is your spirit that is born anew: *"That which is born of the flesh is flesh, and that which is born of the Spirit is spirit"* (John 3:6). Regeneration is the Spirit-wrought renewal of your human spirit, a transforming resuscitation that takes place in this, the very core of your being, so that *"the spirit is alive"* (Rom. 8:10).

So it is your spirit that God has regenerated and

that has been made perfect: *"the spirits of righteous men made perfect"* (Heb. 12:23). But think with me. Your spirit is you. Remember, when your body dies and is placed in the grave, your spirit will ascend to heaven. Your spirit, then, is that part of you which will live forever. Your spirit is the core of your being, the real you. You are a spirit. It is you who has been perfected because your spirit is the real you. Therefore, when God says you have been made forever perfect, He is not speaking figuratively. God is speaking literally—you are perfect.

The Holy Spirit has been joined to your human spirit so that a new spiritual entity has been formed. A new birth has produced a new being. *"Therefore if any man be in Christ, he is a new creature: old things are passed away; behold, all things are become new"* (2 Cor. 5:17 KJV).

A Christian is a person who has become someone he was not before. At conversion, a transformation of your personhood takes place and is evidenced by a new spirituality in outlook, desire, values, and aim.

Furthermore, this metamorphosis so affects your

inner nature that it produces some changes in your performance. No one can become a Christian and not experience some visible changes in his performance. It shall be emphasized, however, that conversion will not effect an instantaneous change in your total performance. The scriptural emphasis is that you should put on, in your outward performance, what you have already become within your inner new self:

> That you be renewed in the spirit of your mind, and put on the new self, which in the likeness of God has been created in righteousness and holiness of the truth.
>
> — Ephesians 4:23–24

Study these words carefully. They say that your new self *"has [already] been created in righteousness and holiness,"* but you must yet *"put on"* this new self in your performance. Your person, now perfect in its regenerated state, will progressively express itself in your performance—as the seed produces an oak tree!

This tells you something else about your person. God has made you forever perfect (see Heb. 10:14). Add this truth as a fourth major aspect of your personal identity and confess it as you read:

- ❖ *"Because of propitiation, I am deeply loved of God."*
- ❖ *"Because of justification, I am fully pleasing to God."*
- ❖ *"Because of reconciliation, I am totally accepted by God."*
- ❖ *"Because of regeneration, I am a new creation, complete in Christ."*

Furthermore, as your person is reflected through your performance, the reflection takes on the hue, color, and tone of your own personality. This is where your individuality comes into play. Your person, having been regenerated in the image of God, will express itself through your performance in a uniqueness and individuality that is characteristic of you alone.

No other life can reflect the glory of God in the

same manner. Due to your salvation, grounded in the four doctrines of propitiation, justification, reconciliation, and regeneration, you are one of a kind—an original—really somebody—a celebrity unsurpassed.

I *have shared these concepts* for many years now. I have noticed that people usually begin to experience a change in their outlook by this point in our study. That is, by the time they have studied through the material contained in the first few chapters, they seem to gain an understanding of our drive for personal significance, our false beliefs about ourselves, and the process by which we can detect them. Your outlook about the future may be brightening with the prospect that there's hope for working through the dark shroud of personal worthlessness that has encompassed you.

Now you have come to recognize the false beliefs about your person that cause your harmful emotions and destructive behavior. The hope for a higher sense of self-worth begins to loom before you. It is at just this point that many have seen a light at the end of the tunnel, only to find out it is a train coming toward them. Your new insight issues into a growing awareness of the powerful false beliefs about yourself, which seem to run right on through you with the force of a railroad train.

The vital fact is that just understanding your false beliefs will not rid you of them. In fact, you might find that you still react the same way to situations. This tendency is so common that some psychologists have a name for it. They call it cognitive-emotive dissonance. Most clients are prone to cognitive-emotive dissonance. This occurs at the point in therapy when clients recognize their irrational beliefs and understand their rational alternative . . . but still feel the same negative ways. These clients see a better way but cannot immediately actualize it, so they conclude they cannot overcome their self-made mess and/or that the principles make no sense.

Pat sobbed uncontrollably for a few minutes. She

had seen how her mind had deceived her and how she was so much more than she had ever thought she was. But knowing this did not free her. It was only over the next several weeks as she learned how to operate against certain specific beliefs that she gained real freedom.

You may recognize your false beliefs, but your harmful emotions are so strong that they continue to control you. You must come against your false beliefs and literally declare war on them to lessen your emotional reaction to them. Paul described this activity as a type of mental warfare when he wrote about the fortresses in our mind:

> We do not war according to the flesh, for the weapons of our warfare are not of the flesh, but divinely powerful for the destruction of fortresses. We are destroying speculations and every lofty thing raised up against the knowledge of God, and we are taking every thought captive to the obedience of Christ.
>
> —2 CORINTHIANS 10:3–5

As we have said, the fortresses Paul referred to here are false beliefs: *"speculations and every lofty thing raised up against the knowledge of God."* The major fortresses are false beliefs about our person. This Scripture mentions weapons of our warfare by which we can destroy the fortresses of false belief. These weapons are not to be confused with the "armor" of the Christian, as discussed in the sixth chapter of Ephesians. The armor of the Christian is for defense. Weapons are for offense. Armor is to protect you from attacks without. Weapons are to overcome fortresses within. The weapons alluded to in 2 Corinthians are weapons of mental warfare by which you conquer the fortresses of your mind.

What are these weapons? Taken in context, the Corinthians would have understood this as reference to the mental attitude of which Paul had spoken a few chapters earlier. This was Paul's follow-up letter to the Corinthians, and they had experienced a great victory over the problems Paul had disclosed in his first letter to them. Several chapters earlier in this epistle, Paul described the mental attitude that led to their change.

They not only felt sorrow for their false beliefs, but they sorrowed to the point of repentance:

> I now rejoice, not that you were made sorrow-
> ful, but that you were made sorrowful to the
> point of repentance; for you were made
> sorrowful according to the will of God, in order
> that you might not suffer loss in anything. . . .
> For the sorrow that is according to the will of
> God produces a repentance without regret.
>
> —2 CORINTHIANS 7:9–10

The tactical method of our mental warfare is to repent. Repentance means to change your mind, thoughts, purpose, and views regarding a matter. It is to have another mind about a thing. To repent of your false beliefs is to change your mind as to what you believe, to recognize your false beliefs as untrue, to reject them, and to replace your false belief with a belief of the truth.

To explain what true repentance is I will use the acronym CROP:

Confession
Reliance
Obedience
Praise

Although this process has a much wider use, here we will focus on rejecting the old identity and living out our new identity. Complete confession is coming into agreement with God in two specific ways. First, we must agree with God specifically about that part of our identity He is bringing to our attention.

God gets our attention in one of three ways. We may see ourselves do something ungodly or destructive and the Holy Spirit convicts us of this sin. We could be screaming at our spouse, lying to someone about something, sitting around morbidly ruminating about what a loser we are, or doing something even worse. In other words, we see something in our behavior, and this includes our mental behavior.

The second way we can detect something's wrong is that our emotions are terribly painful and unproductive. One of the reasons God gave us emotions was to alert us that something is wrong with the beliefs we are basing our lives upon. Usually, we think the emotions are the problem. But if we could take a pill and do away with all such emotions that are painful, we would probably go through life never confronting the false beliefs because we are just too comfortable with ourselves.

The third way we detect false beliefs is to look at the thoughts that are supporting the harmful emotions. My wife, Marilyn, told me one time how God showed her this principle. She had awakened mad about something. Then her attention was diverted by a television show. After a while she realized she wasn't mad anymore and tried to recall what she was mad about in the first place. Emotions die without supportive thoughts to continue giving them life.

CONFESSION

As we ask God to show us whatever He wants to about that which He has brought to our attention, we are going to need to agree with Him about more than the fact that what He is showing us is in our lives. For instance, it is not enough to tell God that you realize that you hate your boss. God wants you to see more about hate in your life than that simple fact. If you will allow Him to do so, God will show you all manner of things about hate in your life that you have long ago forgotten.

God will also show you the destructiveness of (in this case) hate, how it has impacted relationships in your life, and how much control it has in your life; and finally, He will show you what false belief is the root of the hate. You will not be through with this phase until you have come to hate the hate in your life. Then you have seen this as God sees it.

Through all this process you will have continually, verbally declared out loud and to the Lord what He has shown you:

> Lord, I agree with You that this hate is in my life.
> It is sin. I have given authority to hate in my life,
> and this is sin. I have hated, and this has caused
> so many so much pain. I have hated because

people have put me down all my life. For this I forgive them. Their "put-downs" have had their impact because I have believed that who I am is based on what other people think about me. This is a lie I have believed. I have given this lie great authority in my life. This lie is a sin. I hate the hate in my life, and I hate the lie I have believed about myself. I choose to cancel the authority I have given to the hate as well as to the lie about my identity that I have believed. I reject both the hate and the lie. I desire to think Your thoughts.

This is the first half of agreeing with God (confession). Do not rush this part of the process. It is in agreeing with God that the power of sin is removed. But this agreement needs to be honest and complete. The second half is specifically declaring the truth that contradicts the false belief you have believed. Read through the following:

I am deeply loved.

By this the love of God was manifested in us, that God has sent His only begotten Son into the world so that we might live through Him. In this is love, not that we loved God, but that He loved us and sent His Son to be the propitiation for our sins. Beloved, if God so loved us, we also ought to love one another.

—1 JOHN 4:9–11

I am fully pleasing.

Therefore having been justified by faith, we have peace with God through our Lord Jesus Christ.

—ROMANS 5:1

I am totally acceptable and accepted.

And although you were formerly alienated and hostile in mind, engaged in evil deeds, yet He has now reconciled you in His fleshly body through death, in order to present you before Him holy and blameless and beyond reproach.

—COLOSSIANS 1:21–22

I am a new creation, complete in Christ.

And in Him you have been made complete, and
He is the head over all rule and authority.

—COLOSSIANS 2:10

DECLARATION

Because of Christ's redemption,
I am a new creation of infinite worth.
I am deeply loved;
I am completely forgiven;
I am fully pleasing;
I am totally accepted by God.
I am absolutely complete in Christ.
When my performance
Reflects my new identity in Christ;
That reflection is dynamically unique.
There has never been another person
Like me in the history of mankind,
Nor will there ever be.
God has made me an original,
One of a kind, a special person.

Your task will be to confess your personhood until you can believe with full assurance and deep conviction. It will be a difficult and prolonged task to reverse years of false beliefs about your self-concept. Such a confession is a virtual warfare! Your natural tendency will be to hold on to your old identity like a trapeze bar rather than to reach for the new identity God swings your way through Scripture. Confession is a mental weapon of great spiritual value. As used in Scripture, confession means "to agree with God."

As we have said, to confess is to state God's viewpoint about a matter as a declaration of your own viewpoint, and to keep on doing so until you consistently see it just the way God does. The Book of Revelation (12:10–11) speaks of the satanic deception by which Satan deceived the whole world and accuses us all day and night. But the same passage says we can overcome satanic deception by *"the blood of the Lamb"* and *"the word of [our] testimony,"* which is your confession of the truth. Confession is the ultimate weapon with which you storm the fortresses of your mind and bring every thought into obedience to Christ. There are several things to remember:

1. *Confession does not mean your natural mind is in agreement with what you are confessing.* The Bible teaches that the natural mind is antagonistic toward God. It takes spiritual mindedness to renew your natural mind.

> But a natural man does not accept the things of the Spirit of God; for they are foolishness to him, and he cannot understand them, because they are spiritually appraised.
>
> — 1 CORINTHIANS. 2:14

2. *Remember you are confessing the truth of Scripture, so you will need to saturate your mind with the scriptural basis for the four confessions.* Memorize the passages. Study them exhaustively. Meditate on them. Your faith in these four confessions will come from the convincing nature of the Word of God itself: *"So faith comes from hearing, and hearing by the word of Christ"* (Rom. 10:17).

3. *Confess the truth of your personal worth with regard to*

definite false beliefs as they relate to a particular situation. Ask God to show you which of these verses or even other verses He wants you to declare.

4. *As you confess, take the time to think through the truth of the fourfold confession about your personhood as it relates to specific false beliefs.*

5. *It is not the unthinking, mechanical utterances of these confessions, but your conscious realization of the logic of the truth they contain that changes your mind about your false beliefs as you confess who you are and reason through the scriptural basis for your confession.*

For example, as you confess, "I am deeply loved of God," think through the doctrine of propitiation found in 1 John 4:9–10. If God Almighty loved you enough to deliver His Son up to death for your sake, you are certainly loved of God.

In summary, not only must you detect and reject your false beliefs about your self-worth, but you must also correct your false beliefs with the four confessions of your worth as a Christ person.

As you make these declarations, you are speaking God's will and truth over your life. In doing this, you are beginning to experience what it means to rule as part of your new identity.

Ask God to lead you in what to declare about yourself as reflected in the above. You are to do this after you have agreed with God about that from which you need to be set free.

RELIANCE

We rely on whatever identity reflects our beliefs about ourselves. It matters little if these beliefs are from Adam, Satan, or God as to whether these beliefs impact our lives. Lies as well as the truth have the same ability to shape our experience of life. So as we consider living life based on what God has declared about us, we are going to be in a real battle. Our minds, which are antagonistic toward God and the things of God, will battle us.

> That, in reference to your former manner of life,
> you lay aside the old self, which is being
> corrupted in accordance with the lusts of deceit,
> and that you be renewed in the spirit of your
> mind, and put on the new self, which in the
> likeness of God has been created in righteous-
> ness and holiness of the truth.
>
> —EPHESIANS 4:22–24

Lay off, put aside, do not operate in the old self. The old self has the following characteristics:

* ❖ It is being corrupted with the lusts of deceit (Eph. 4:22–24).
* ❖ It has evil practices (Col. 3:9).
* ❖ It has our body of sin (Rom. 6:6).

Put on, operate in the new self. The new self has the following characteristics:

* ❖ It has been created in the likeness of God in righteousness and holiness (Eph. 4:22–24).

❖ It has been strengthened according to God's riches (Eph. 3:16).

❖ It is the temple of the Holy Spirit (1 Cor. 6:19).

❖ It knows the thoughts of man (1 Cor. 2:11).

❖ It is the dwelling place of Christ (Eph. 3:17).

❖ It is the new creation, the real you (2 Cor. 5:17).

The new self is all we shall experience when we enter heaven; therefore, it obviously carries with it all the capabilities we shall need once we get there. It also has all the abilities. Unfortunately, we are used to living in the old man, thinking with the old mind and experiencing the old emotions and habit patterns. It is within this understanding that we must comprehend what the Bible calls "reckoning."

Scripture clearly teaches that the new man has the capability of reckoning death to the old man and all that is associated with him. The new man also has the power to reckon himself alive to, and therefore experience the reality of, being the new creation.

In our process, reckoning is used in the following two steps.

First, in order to utilize the rejection-confession response, you have to short-circuit actions building on other actions. Our minds are so fouled up with false beliefs that if God had not given us the power to reckon, we would not have enough time and tranquility to experience renewing of our minds. As soon as the thoughts have us at the emoting stage, reactions can occur quickly. As soon as action occurs, the beliefs are reinforced (energized) even more, the thoughts come more quickly, the emotions are stronger, and action builds upon action.

This is most dramatic with depression. A person experiences an actual or feared failure or rejection (situation), which triggers the false beliefs (belief) and the "down" emotions. Soon the person is contemplating how bad he or his condition (action) is. His contemplating how bad off he is reinforces the false beliefs, which makes him feel even worse.

God gave us reckoning to short-circuit this process. Because of our union with Christ, we can experience the emotion, but not act upon it. In the example, reckoning would mean we would not let ourselves contemplate how bad everything is. It's painful. The "death to self" associated with reckoning is not pleasurable. But it is effective.

Reckoning is not as painful as giving in to your enemy, the old self. Face it. You are going to experience pain. It will be either the pain of refusing a temptation or the pain associated with the giving in to the old self. Reckoning ourselves dead to emotions does not mean we ignore the fact that the emotions exist.

Reckoning is meant to be used only long enough for mind renewal to occur. It is taught wrongly as the final tool for the Christian. I've seen many Christians have a horrible existence because they would reckon, reckon, and then fail. This pattern would continue until they would give up. It is not that reckoning does not work; it is just not the last step.

The second step of reckoning is this: With most Christians, what the mind believes to be true has the authority in their lives. What their minds tell them to do, they do. What their minds tell them is true or real, they accept as fact. What their emotions motivate them toward, they go for. This places the mind in conflict with the Lordship of Jesus. The mind, which has many unrenewed areas, is to be subservient to the authority of the Holy Spirit as He directs us through our human spirit.

OBEDIENCE

Obedience is the next process in our CROP explanation. God gives us opportunities to be obedient to demonstrate all that He has done in our lives. Being given the opportunity to live based on the truth, as compared to all the times we have lived based on a false belief, provides us an opportunity to seal the truth into our lives.

The three areas of obedience are our thoughts, our reactions, and our exposure. First, we will be given the opportunity to guard our thoughts. If we allow our minds to think thoughts we know have as their basis the lies we have believed about ourselves, then we are back to relying on a lie. Someone harshly criticizes you. You now have an opportunity to receive that criticism of your person or reject it.

A small child has learned to say the word *loser*. This child comes up to you and repeats this word over and over again. You can see how you could reject that term as applying to you. However, if someone you know tells you that you are a loser, it gets to you. Why? Does the age of someone make a lie the truth? No! No one has the right to devalue you at any time, and you do not have the right to accept that term as truth about yourself.

Second, we must look to be obedient in our reactions. This means we do not allow ourselves to act upon our thoughts if we have not guarded our thoughts well and they are creating all manner of destructive emotions within us. For instance, you may be angry with your boss for his harshness, but you do not necessarily quit your job because you have not constrained your thinking and you are extremely angry. We need to commit ourselves not to decide anything important while certain emotions are pounding within us.

Finally, we can see patterns within our lives where we make sure that we do not expose ourselves to rejection or failure. This both isolates us as well as limits what we can do in our lives. For us to be obedient, sometimes we must push ourselves into situations we have avoided in the past.

As we begin to realize that God has set us free from the bondage of the old identity, we will indeed praise Him. Heaven will be full of praise. Why? It will not be because someone works us into praise or because we get caught up in what others are doing. We will praise Him because we will clearly see what He has done for us.

This praise need not wait until heaven. But praise will not happen here the way it should until our thoughts reflect God's thoughts. All other praise is shallow manipulation and an attempt to gain some emotional experience.

"Fake it till you make it" cannot be found anywhere in Scripture. If praise is not coming from you as a response to what God is doing in your life, ask God to show you what is wrong. Once the reality of your new identity begins to take root in your life, praise will flow from you.

Let us look at Sue. She came to see how her anger was caused by the pain she experienced from the sense of failure and rejection. She also recognized that pain was due to her false beliefs. Now she would have to declare war. These were her declarations:

> I have a belief that I must be adequate in order to feel good about myself. My mind tells me I'm a real loser and that I'm a failure. All of this is a lie. I agree I failed in my performance when I criticized Bill and refused to have anything to do with him. However, that is my

performance. That is not my person, but a reflection of the deception, which is still within my mind.

Instead of accepting that this or any performance could depreciate me, I choose to believe I am a fully pleasing person for I am fully pleasing to God (Rom. 5:1): "Therefore, having been justified by faith, we have peace with God through our Lord Jesus Christ."

Here we see Sue using rejection of the false beliefs and then confession of the truth:

My mind cannot grasp how God does this. I choose to be free from my mind dictating reality to me. I will to believe I am deeply loved of God as seen in 1 John 4:9–10: "By this the love of God was manifested in us, that God has sent His only begotten Son into the world so that we might live through Him. In this is love, not that we loved God, but that He loved us and sent

His Son to be the propitiation for our sins."

I realize that Bill and my mother hold less of an opinion of me than God does. I choose to reject their opinion of me and to accept that I am totally accepted by God as Colossians 1:21–22 says: "Although you were formerly alienated and hostile in mind, engaged in evil deeds, yet He has now reconciled you in His fleshly body through death, in order to present you before Him holy and blameless and beyond reproach."

"My feelings tell me I am not a wonderful, accepted, loved person. My feelings tell me I'm a dumb failure who ought to punish myself by even killing myself. My feelings are based on a lie I believe about myself. I reject those feelings as having any authority in my life.

I am therefore not only rejecting the opinion Bill and my mother have of me, but I choose to relate to them as God would have me. I need not retaliate, as I have not allowed them to hurt me.

Finally, I praise God that He has worked

with me so long and in such grace. I will wake up with praise on my lips and lie down overflowing with thanksgiving.

If the false beliefs remain in our mind unchallenged and without being rejected, they retain their unconscious influence and cause further wrong reactions at every similar situation in the future. For example, a religious counselor might have told Sue her problem was that she was wrong, that she needed to confess her sinful behavior, and that she also harbored resentment toward her mother and husband, which she should confess. Such a counselor would exhort her to confess her wrongdoing and resentment, pray, and change her behavior.

If Sue confessed her wrong attitude about her husband and her mother, she would probably feel some immediate relief and feel somewhat better about herself. At least she would have accepted the responsibility for her actions. However, if this is all Sue does, she will still harbor the unconscious false beliefs about her personal worth, the satanic deception that really caused her harmful emotions and destructive behavior in the first place. Sue would be able to change her behavior only temporarily; then she would probably fall back into the same behavior pattern again and take on compounded guilt for her failure. No, Sue needed a change of mind about her specific false beliefs. She not only repented of her wrongdoing and wrong feeling toward her husband and her mother, but more important, Sue also repented about the fact that she harbored the false beliefs that caused those feelings. These false beliefs were her problem, and she declared war on them. She began to reject them and to refuse to live her life based on them.

The first weapon of repentance, then, is to reject your false beliefs each time they affect you. In its essence, warfare is a sustained and continuous battle. Let every disturbing situation be your opportunity to focus upon the false beliefs that affect you. Do this again and again, in all types of problematic situations, until you become acutely conscious of them. This lifts your false beliefs from your unconscious into your conscious awareness, enabling you to confront them more directly and consistently, and to come against them more forcefully. Soon you will be waging a conscious and constant warfare in rejection of your false beliefs; and this is what it takes to reverse years of habitual wrong thinking.

Rita had a dominating false belief that she must take the blame and pay for any shortcoming in her performance in order to feel good about herself. She felt bad about herself in any disagreement with her opinionated husband and for every failure of her irresponsible children. Rita began to detect and reject her false belief, but she did not begin to experience deliverance until she began to reason through her four confessions as she declared them. "After all," she reasoned, "a person who is unconditionally loved, fully pleasing, totally accepted, and a new creation in the eyes of God has no business feeling bad about herself or taking on condemnation."

It was Rita's confession and her understanding of

the truth of these confessions that delivered her from self-condemnation. Oh, she continued to take full responsibility for the results of her own actions. But she refused to take personal condemnation, to hate herself, or to feel that she deserved to be punished for her faults or failures. Rita did not allow her mind to ruminate on any of these things. She learned to praise God for all He had done in her life.

Art's false beliefs included an obsession with gaining recognition. However, when Art began to confess his worth in God's eyes, he began to think through the truth of the four confessions. He studied the Scriptures on which they are based, and he began to realize that he was indeed a loved child of God. The change in Art's life was evidenced in more self-assurance. He realized his acceptance as a person, so he no longer had to expend so much energy evoking affirmation of his personal worth from everyone else. Art became much more relaxed and open. He became more warm and spontaneous in his relationships. He learned to listen and consider the opinions of others.

Art became excited about learning all it means to be a new creation. When he went to church, Art sang praises with heartfelt abandonment.

In a short while, all of us who are in Christ will be released from this body of sin and begin forever in heaven with a new body and a soul that no longer carries the burden of the Fall. The only thing that will be the same will be our spirit. The same spirit we have right now, which forms the basis of our new identity, will rule our soul and body.

Faith will be no more because everything will be sight. We will see Jesus as He is. We will clearly know all that He accomplished when He bought Salvation for us. We will know Him and we will know ourselves. We will truly experience the abundant life.

Yet, Christ does not want us to wait until heaven. The Holy Spirit is more than willing to bring that abundant life springing forth within us.

The only question left is, What will be your story? Will you continue living in the old identity or find the freedom and destiny Christ's death provides for you?

Perhaps the following prayer will help you begin to discover your new identity:

My Father, who is in heaven, You are holy; therefore, I depend completely upon what You have declared to be truth in spite of what my mind tells me. Rule my heart and mind so that the will that is reflected in heaven will be reflected here on earth in my life.

Jesus, thank You for all that You went through for me. I want to honor You for what You did for me by completely embracing the truths found in justification, reconciliation, regeneration, and propitiation. I desire You to search me and show me where I have given authority to the evil one by believing his lies. Make me aware when I am responding to false beliefs. I choose to forgive others because of the great forgiveness You have given me. Until I see You face to face, I desire to live by the power You give me and in response to Your Word. Amen.

TO LEARN HOW TO BETTER IMPLEMENT
THE PRINCIPLES IN
The Secret of Significance,
YOU WILL WANT
The Search for Significance Book/Workbook.

In this book, you will:

- Find a more in-depth explanation of the truths found in *The Secret of Significance*

- Gain new skills for getting off the performance treadmill

- Discover, through self-inventory exercises, how the four False Beliefs have negatively impacted your life

- Learn how to overcome obstacles that prevent you from experiencing the truth that your self-worth is found only in the love, acceptance, and forgiveness of Christ

- Be led through an extensive, application-driven workbook that has changed the lives of countless people

You can find freedom that will last your lifetime-freedom for which Christ has already paid the price. Now it's time for you to walk in the light of truth.

W PUBLISHING GROUP

ROBERT S. McGEE

0-8499-4092-3